Poetry of Peisse

CREATION STORY

Sharon Cully

WHERE WE ARE NOW

Copyright © 2015 Sharon Cully

The moral right of Sharon Cully to be identified as the Author of the work and Emma Jarvis as the Artist has been asserted by them in accordance with the Copyright, Designs and Patents Act 1988. All rights reserved. No part of this book may be used or reproduced by any means, graphic, electronic, or mechanical, including photocopying, recording, taping or by any information storage retrieval system without the written permission of the publisher except in the case of brief quotations embodied in critical articles and reviews.

National Library of Australia Cataloguing-in-Publication entry
Author: Cully, Sharon, author.
Title: Poetry of Peisse : creation story / Sharon Cully ; Emma Jarvis, illustrator.
ISBN: 978-0-9923653-5-6 (paperback)
ISBN: 978-0-9923653-7-0 (hardback)
ISBN: 978-0-9923653-8-7 (ebook)
Subjects: Creation--Poetry.
Other Authors/Contributors: Jarvis, Emma, illustrator.
Dewey Number: A821.4

Publishing Imprint: Piesse Publishing

Publishing Details
Published in Australia

Printed & Channel Distribution:
Lightning Source USA/UK/AUS/EUR

For further exploration any of the material contained within this book the following contact details have been provided:

Author:	Sharon Cully. Where We Are Now Past and Future.
	and Piesse Publishing.
Author Web Site:	www.wherewearenow.com.au
Email:	peisse246@gmail.com

Acknowledgements

No collection of words is complete without the acknowledgement of those who have supported the process. Thanks must go to my family who have supported and loved me throughout all these times in my life. They have always helped me to climb up the ladder again.

My husband Peter deserves a special mention for his belief and support in me even during the challenging moments.

Thanks must go to my special group also on their own unique journey who, for a number of years, meet with me weekly. Their support, encouragement and at times humour, keep me going.

Above all I give my thanks to God, who has stayed with me on every moment of my journey making sure I am never alone.

Communique Of Our Journey

I seemed to have been born into this world with an inbuilt "Knowing" that we are here for a bigger purpose than we can see with our eyes. Evidence surrounds us that there is a powerful Creator.

Life could not just have made itself to this level of incredible detail and complexity by itself. Evolution just didn't sufficiently explain why we are so different to the other creatures on Earth. All other animals seem to spend most of their life growing, reproducing successfully and then dying. It is almost as if they seem to only live to procreate and then to die.

Humans are different. We do all those things but in addition, we strive to better ourselves. We have a consciousness that leads us to create, invent, imagine and even tear down. We spend a entire lifetime working to improve ourselves. We get to the stage where we finally think we have worked life out. We learn lots of things including the development of wisdom, compassion, discernment, understanding, self-control, patience and tolerance. Then….we die!

What? We bury everything that we finally have learnt? What on earth was the point of that? Somehow, to me life seems back to front. When we get to the end of our life only then, do we finally work out what we were supposed to have worked out at the beginning.

When the end comes we often haven't managed to accomplish all the good we have finally learnt. We suddenly feel like we haven't been able to fit it all in. The end of our life looms too quick.

I have always known that there must be more to life. There must be a purpose and a game plan. There must be a bigger strategy behind our existence. Otherwise, why would we try to advance ourselves beyond mere survival? Instead we could do like most other creations just grow, reproduce and then, die.

This "Knowing" was intensified as I studied the heavens and the earth. Then, I studied the complexity of all life forms on the earth and discovered that not a single thing could happen by chance. The simple acts of seeing, hearing, touch, movement and sensation are staggering, to name but a few. If these things were not made totally correct the first time, then we would not have survived at all. How could we have survived blind, deaf, without sensation or movement control?

I have experienced events in my life that could not be explained in any way by human efforts to quantify them with science. These events increased my feelings of awareness and knowing. I didn't have to hear or see to Believe. I could feel it! I continue to experience it!

TABLE OF CONTENTS

Sun

Creation

Life

Wind

Earth

Clouds

Water

Moon

You And Me

This is my painting of a crab nebular. It shows the creation of the stars. The explosion of star dust across the void that provides the building blocks of all Creation and Life.

POETRY OF PEISSE
Creation Story

Sun

So bright, intense and hot;
holding all stardust close in Creation's cot.
Every ingredient and element is there to see;
everything, even the beginnings of you and me.

A moment in time too far;
there would be no big creation shout, Hoorah.
A moment in time too near;
the result would be only cinders and fear.

Precision, perfection, nothing ever wrong;
mathematics talks volumes through song.
The language of the stars is visible there;
creation's formula of Life to share.

This wisdom is not hidden or rare;
simply, we need to have those who choose to care.
Those who search for answers with an open mind;
seeking the truth, daring to share it with all mankind.

The truth will set us free;
showing the origins of you and me.
This will stop all war and separation;
you will see we are all parts of one great nation.

We are one, me, you and all the others;
all of creation has mothers, fathers, sisters and brothers.
Earth people, star people, plant and animal;
all are one at a very primordial level.

Rocks, earth, crystals, energy and light;
all are created and work to unite.
They too have the same will to aspire;
coming from the sun's great central fire.

Earth, water, wind and fire;
elements that help life rise from the mire.
To survive and to be truly free;
because we are all one, you, them and me.

Creation

Sun was there before the story of life began;
saw life start, crawl and watched as it ran.
Sun felt pride, pleasure and contentment;
as from the void was released all the firmament.

The land and oceans moved in a dance;
beginning a very long romance.
There they clung together refusing to be torn;
enabling them to give this world form.

Sun smiled and was glad;
all elements and building blocks of life the sun had.
Together they burst forth at the right time;
in the right sequence, like a melodious rhyme.

Light, warmth and love without measure;
binding all these ingredients into beautiful treasure.
Stirred with the right amount of movement and harmony;
life burst forth like a tumultuous symphony.

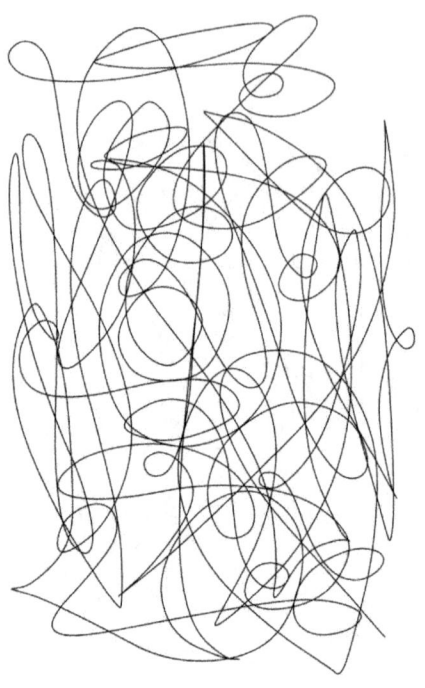

LIFE

Our whole earth is alive;
being near her makes all my senses strive.
The plants and animals upon her thrive;
those who exist are more than one million and five.

A web of relationships exist;
hiding from view as though in a mist.
Insects, spiders and flees;
the tall, the small and even trees.

The tiny ones may chirp;
larger ones may slurp.
The hungry ones watch and moan;
as over the silent night hilltops they roam.

All are aware of this wondrous life we share;
aware of the combined need to care.
Respect that is the key;
between every living thing, you and me.

But Life does not necessarily have to physically move;
neither will it have to hip hop or groove.
Rather, it is a Presence there;
something or somewhat of which, I am aware.

This persistent feeling that I am known;
that others watch to see how I have grown.
They share all my moments of triumph and glee;
watching as I grow and learnt to be me.

Wind

Wind often touches my face;
sometimes pummelling me as if I disgrace.
But usually, softly, my skin is stroked;
I know the feel of her, but her presence is cloaked.

I feel the Wind's vibrancy and life;
her ability to wander through places wrought with strife.
To travel across oceans and lands;
across mountains and red desert sands.

Don't be fooled the Wind is alive and free;
she feels and has emotions just like you and me.
She tells us the story;
of humanities past and future glory.

Wind lets out a gentle call;
telling me of other past civilisations.
About their rise and falls;
where once stood castles and kingdoms with mighty halls.

They once stood with Pride, Love and Grace;
but now the past, present and future begin to race.
They trip over each other in their haste;
hungering for more life a sample just to taste.

It's a race that tells of the rise and fall;
of handsome gladiators and kingdoms that stood tall.
Their reign passed like winds over desert sands;
telling us this, the wind reaches out her hands.

Notice the gentle touch of the Wind;
caressing all of me as to the heaven she will ascend.
To tell of Earth's great creation story;
all of it, the grief and the glory.

Wind spirit is our counsellor and friend;
alerting us to issues that we ought to tend.
She passes over all the lands and the ocean;
gathering up all our emotion.

Wind wipes our emotional slate clean;
scrubbing, scrubbing but seldom seen.
Incognito the Wind wipes clean our Earth;
removing debris, anger or tickling us with mirth.

Earth

Earth on which I stand;
is more than a sphere of sand.
Rather she is a nurturing and loving mother;
feeding, protecting and loving me like no other.

There is a pulsating throb of life;
I feel it through my feet and heart all my life.
Do I stop to listen?
Do I bother to discover what I am miss'en?

Earth provides caverns for creatures to hide;
crevices and meadows in which life can reside.
Roads and paths are etched to guide feet;
collecting and moving all life to where the ends meet.

The grasses clothe her nakedness;
plants and flowers grip tightly her crevices.
The trees protect and support her vulnerability;
rocks help cover her wounds and her humility.

How we pry and poke into Earth's face;
forgetting she sustains us and every other race.
Raped, pillaged and treated like dirt;
forgetting about her feelings, emotions and hurt.

Man goes deep into the belly of our Earth;
forgetting her feeling within that ample girth.
Man smashes and steals her treasure;
taking more than his fair measure.

Is this how you would treat your mother?
She gives all, to you, and every other.
Water, air, earth and fire;
everything freely given so life can fulfil its desire.

Treat her gently and with great care;
as she sustains this web of life for us all to share.
Look where you walk and feel her skin;
opening her arms wide she encourages you in.

Clouds

Clouds with their many faces;
thunderous or slender with delicate traces.
Colours painted in pastels or bolds;
causing us to tremble with pleasure as their story unfolds.

Beautiful, regal, towering or wispy fine;
flat or jagged like a distant cliff line.
They provide shade, love and protection;
sprinkling waters upon us all like a benediction.

WATER

Our Earth's partner, a slippery friend;
clings to Earth's skin and to her wounds will tend.
The waters soothe, warm, caress and bathe;
as Earth flinches and hurts as if cut by a lathe.

Water absorbs our mess and pollution;
creating a buffering soup of protection.
Water dilutes hate, dissent, it bathes and gathers;
circling us all, it feels like the arms of our mothers.

Water the womb of all creation;
pulsing with life, love and an open invitation.
For us to finally live and let live;
learning instead to love, forgive and above all, to give.

Moon

Moon shines down, watching over his Earth friend;
wondering if her trials will reach even to him in the end.
For now, he sends abounding light, energy and love;
providing a balm for feelings bruised, down from above.

Moon radiates the night sky;
rarely we wonder why.
He supervises everything from on high;
watching all of life, you and I.

Moon works closely with his friend, Oceans;
soothing the Earth and absorbing wild emotions.
Absorbing Life's mess;
softening Life's blows, emotions and stress.

This is done on behalf of all creation;
continuing to let life exist with its varied manifestation.
Hoping beyond hope that we figure it out;
before we open Pandora's Box and let all the forces out.

Forces that provide great freedom and knowledge;
wrongly used turn everything to a porridge.
A cauldron, a melting pot holds it all;
as life as we know it slowly starts to slide and fall.

Such decline once started is impossible to reverse;
and this beautiful world could become a curse.
By taking with her everything we have ever known;
reverting life here back to other times renown.

Moon's many faces;
have watched the rise and fall of many races.
Moon loves life and wants us to finally see;
survival starts and ends, with just you and me.

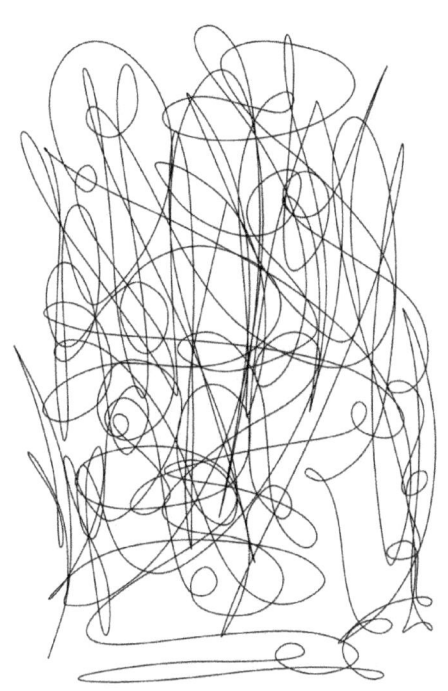

You And Me

Now aware of the great responsibility we share;
armed with the Truth we will avoid Fate's snare.
Instead, Love, Truth and Healing we will share;
showing the world how to truly love and care.

Sharon Cully

Since 1974 I have worked in the Health Care Industry as a Registered Nurse and then in Government and Non-Government Health Service Management. I was also employed to manage systems (Accreditation and Risk Management) in the Public Sector. I have been an Aged Care Assessor, Aged Care Facility Manager, Teacher and Workplace Assessor. This has provided me with extensive experience in the management of people through all types of life traumas and crises. My experience ranges across many cultures and all age groups. My life has been one of service to others and continues to still be.

On a personal level I have lived through many of the same crises that affect those I care for. I have lived through death, grief, bereavement and chronic illness. These have added additional levels of understanding, empathy and insight into the needs of others. Importantly, combined, it provided me the best training ground to assist others who now experience these issues themselves.

As a child I emigrated from England to Australia with my parents. This taught me about isolation. These difficulties are faced by all others when removed from their social and family support systems. The traumatic death of my first husband at a very young age caused me to experience an "Out of Body Experience" (OBE) and so began many other metaphysical/ paranormal events throughout my life.

My second husband taught me a different journey of self-understanding, self-worth, roles, social stigma and most importantly the inner strength that all humans are capable of finding in adversity. The most important lesson learnt is that there is no such word as "can't". An escape to the country from an urban upbringing saw the development of skills related to survival on the land, farming and self-sufficiency. It also taught the true meaning of severe physical and financial hardship.

I have travelled extensively to different areas of our world. I have lived and worked in urban, rural and remote areas. This has taught me to wonder and love our world with all its diversity of environments and people. Difficult and far reaching personal and professional experiences have caused me to search and question the meaning of Life. I reached out and searched for God. I searched for the reasons why "bad things happen to good people". I read profusely and this includes books on philosophy, theology, psychology, astrology, archaeology, quantum healing, reflexology, bio energy fields, healing crystals, and all manner of alternative therapies. (This is only to name a few). My library is extensive.

In 2014 I was successful in publishing the Where We Are Now Series Volume 1 and 2 of Inspirational Poetry. I am a public speaker and spiritual healer. I dabble in art and am a capable musician. Most of all I love to immerse myself in nature and find solace on my property called Peisse.

Emma Jarvis

There have been many experiences I have encountered and endured in my short life. At times it feels as if I have lived many lives in this one lifetime. I have had many unexplained health symptoms and discomforts to accompany my days.

I experienced the type of ill health that resulted in the complete devolvement from a strong and independent woman to a frail one. Not only physically but also of mind and emotion. I was so destroyed that total dependence on another was essential. The type of ill health that saw me curled up crying to God for help when the pain and discomfort could no longer be endured.

Feeling disappointed and abandoned by the medical world I went searching for answers elsewhere. I found spirituality. I found more questions and I found myself. This search went on for some 5 years. I was led on a journey of true self-discovery and healing of so many facets. It was on one of these many paths that this journey directed me to a meditation class in the March of 2011. My hand began to tremble and shake. This was the beginning of something very new for me. It was also the beginning of my climb back to health and a new way to help myself, Mother Earth and one day others. Information was coming through my hand in the form of Multidimensional Energy Patterns.

It is these patterns which accompany and support the wonderful healing words contained within this book. I hope they bring you as much comfort and strength as I have personally received from them.

The patterns are intricate, some simplistic others complex. However, what is behind each one is the ability of movement brought through your hand as a cycle of frequency to build upon and sustain the energy of the Being or the land for whom it has been drawn. So these are sustainable energy patterns that bring back their original energy that have been compromised in some way by their own thinking processes, by the energy interaction of others or by what we will call war-like disputes for the land. The land holds memory just as your cells hold memory.

So your energy patterns sustain and create the origination of energy so that it can be grasped, integrated and utilised for them to move forward. To offer this to Humanity at this time is more than appropriate. For what is occurring on the Earth plane right now in relation to the change of the geometry of the grids, is a paradigm that will collapse everything that you have considered to be an ongoing, control structure.

www.ingramcontent.com/pod-product-compliance
Lightning Source LLC
Chambersburg PA
CBHW062244300426
44110CB00034B/1923